BRITISH REGIONAL SLANG

A POCKET GUIDE TO UK WORDS & PHRASES

So you don't look stupid
when trying to understand
Brits

PREFACE

The UK features unusual accents and pronunciations of both vowels and consonants. To make matters worse, certain regions have developed a unique vocabulary which can be utterly mystifying to outsiders. This mini illustrated 'dictionary' of words and expressions from the United Kingdom is here to rescue you.

ALREET!

0121

Birmingham

Birmingham dialing code.

Used to tell someone to get lost. 01 do one.

"Can I have some of your chocolate?"
"0121 mate."

AAL

Newcastle / Sunderland

All.

"This book is aal aboot British words."

NEWCASTLE

AH SURE LOOK

Ireland

Used as a conversation killer or a way to say what the f**k can we do about it.

"And he died."
"Ah sure look."

AHT

Yorkshire

Out.

"We're going aht tonight for a drink."

ALREET

Newcastle / Sunderland

Greeting. Alright!

"Alreet mate, what ya uptee the morra?"

AN ALL

Yorkshire

As well.

"It was that cold the sheep were shivering an all."

ANG ON A MO

Liverpool

Please wait a moment.

"Ang on a mo Nathan, Emma will let you stay out another ten minutes."

ARL ARSE

Liverpool

A word to describe somebody
who is being mean.

"Don't be an arl arse Emma."

ARR AY

Liverpool

Expression of disbelief.
I can't believe you just did that.

"Arr ay, that was arl arse Nathan."

ASK ME BOLLOCKS

Ireland

An effective way for a male to make clear you're not answering to their request.

"Can you lend me a tenner?"
"Ask me bollocks."

AYE

Yes.

"Emma said aye to a kiss behind the shed."

AYE RIGHT

Scotland

Expressing disbelief.

"She said that? Aye right."

BAB

Birmingham

An endearing term for a
female. Brummie for hun/babe.

*"Thanks for driving me to the Bullring
bab."*

BABBI

Yorkshire

Baby.

"Nathan stop crying like a babbi."

BALTIC

Liverpool

Freezing.

"I wouldn't wear a skirt today Emma, it's baltic out there."

BAMPOT

Scotland

Idiot.

"The bampot messaged me again."

BANG

Ireland

A terrible smell.

"The bang on Nathan would be able sink the titanic."

BANJOED

Ireland

Hungover.

"Ah stop, I'm banjoed."

BARM

Liverpool

A bread roll (bap or bun).

"Gimme that barm Nathan, I'm hungry."

BASICALLY

Preface used for everything.

"Basically, I don't like her. Basically."

BEAUT

Liverpool

An idiot.

"You're a beaut Nathan, do one."

BECK

Yorkshire

A stream.

"Emma said she's off for a dip in't beck."

BE REET

Yorkshire

It will be ok.

"Don't worry about Emma, she'll be reet."

BEVVY

An alcoholic beverage.

"Shall we go for a bevvy la?"

BEZZIE

Liverpool / Manchester

Best friend.

"Emma is my bezzie."

BIFTER

Liverpool

Cigarette or a joint.

"Give us some of that bifter lad."

BIG MASSIVE

Wales

Huge.

"I don't want to fight Nathan, he's big massive!"

BIRD

Scotland

A girl or girlfriend.

"*Say hello to my new bird, Emma.*"

BLACK STUFF

Ireland

Irish dry stout, Guinness.

"Back in work in an hour so get in only four pints of the black stuff for me."

BLEEDIN'

Ireland

A word to emphasize anything, good or bad.

"I'm bleedin' p*ssed off with you Nathan."

BLUE

Manchester

A Manchester City supporter.

"I've always been a blue."

BOBBY DAZZLER

Newcastle

Something or someone excellent.

> *"Did you see that girl? What a bobby dazzler!"*
> *"That's Emma."*

BOG

Yorkshire

Toilet.

"Had far too many sausages for breakfast, I'm going t' bog."

BONNIE

Newcastle/ Sunderland / Scotland

Good looking.

"Nathan is a bonnie lad."

BOSS

Liverpool

Cool, good, brilliant, fantastic, great, ace, wonderful, sound.

"Did you see that chick? She's boss!"

BROON

Newcastle

Brown.

Newcastle Brown Ale.

"A bottle o' broon please mate."

BRUMMIE

A resident of Birmingham. Also the Birmingham accent.

"He's a true Brummie, born in Brum with the accent."

BUTTY

Liverpool / Yorkshire

Sandwich.

"Just get us a ham butty la."

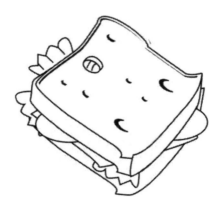

BUZZ

Birmingham

The mode of public transport every other English speaker calls a bus.

"The buzz is never on time."

BUZZING

Wales

Happy, excited OR something smells really bad.

"This place is brilliant, I'm buzzing."

BYE BYE BYE

One bye just isn't enough.

"Bye, bye, bye."

CANNY

Newcastle/ Sunderland

Used to describe something good.

"Emma's car is canny like."

CARGO

Scotland

Alcohol bought from an off-licence to be consumed at home. Common in Glasgow.

"Did you see the amount of cargo Kevin bought?!"

CHAMPION

Yorkshire

Amazing.

"Last night's kebab was champion."

CHEERS PET

Newcastle

Thank you.

"Pass me bait Emma, cheers pet."

CHIP

Go.

"Let's chip Emma, it's boring here."

CHIPPER

Ireland

Fish and chip shop.

"Can't wait for a chipper tonight."

CHOCKA

Liverpool

Busy.

"Don't go that way, it's chocka there."

CHUFFED

Yorkshire

Happy. Pleased.

"Emma was chuffed with Nathan's results."

CLAMMING

Newcastle/ Sunderland

Feeling so hungry.

"Am clamming, get me to the nearest Greggs asap."

C'MERE TILL
I TELL YA

Ireland

I have something to tell you.

"C'mere till I tell ya. There's a mouse in the house."

COUNCIL POP

Birmingham

Tap water.

"Need some council pop for my hangover."

COZZIE

Liverpool

Swimming costume.

"See Nathan, my cozzie still fits me."

CRABBIT

Scotland

Grumpy or miserable.

"Why are you so crabbit today?"

CRACKING

Wales

Excellent.

"The dessert was cracking."

CRAIC

Fun / gossip.

"What's the craic Nathan?"

CRIMBO

Liverpool

Christmas.

> *"I still need to get me ma her prezzie for Chrimbo!"*

C'UNT

Yorkshire

Could not.

"I c'unt see past Emma's behind."

DAFTY

Scotland

Stupid, silly or foolish.

"Stop pulling that face you dafty."

DALES

Yorkshire Dales.

"*Nathan is off for a reet long walk in the Dales at weekend for some peace from Emma.*"

DEADLY

Ireland

Brilliant, fantastic.

"That was a deadly film."

DEEK

Newcastle/ Sunderland

To have a quick look at something.

"Have a deek at that bonny lass."

DELIRA & EXIRA

Ireland

Delighted & excited.

"I'm delira and excira to meet the dog."

DE POOL

Liverpool

De = The, Pool = Liverpool.
Scouse way of saying Liverpool.

"Nathan is deffo not from de Pool!"

DID I 'ECKERS LIKE

Yorkshire

No I did not.

"Did I 'eckers like eat the last Yorkshire pudding."

DINNIT

Sunderland

Don't.

"I dinnit know like."

DIVVENT

Newcastle

Don't.

> *"What divvent you know Nathan."*
> *"I divvent know like."*

DIVVY

Liverpool / Newcastle

Generic insult. Stupid or silly.

"What a divvy Nathan is."

DOPE

Ireland

A stupid person.

"The dope Nathan put salt in my tea instead of sugar."

DRIVE

Wales

A bus driver or taxi driver.

"Thanks for the lift Drive."

DRYSHITE

Ireland

Someone who is really boring.

"Nathan is an awful dryshite."

DUDS

Manchester

Underpants.

"Anyone seen my duds?"

'ECK

Yorkshire

Heck (dropping the H at the beginning).
Hell.

"Flippin' 'eck, Emma's gorgeous."

EEE

Liverpool

An expression of disgust or disapproval.

"Look what Emma is wearing. Eee!"

EEE

Newcastle / Sunderland

An expression usually at the start of the sentence often used just for the hell of it.

"Eee man, you'll never guess who I saw down the toon today. Emma!"

EEE BY GUM

Yorkshire

Oh my god.

"Eee by gum! Get that spider out of the house Nathan!"

EEJIT

Ireland / Scotland

A friendly harmless idiot.

"Check that eejit over there."

ENTRY

Liverpool

An alleyway.

"Nathan was with those scallies walking down the entry before."

EY UP

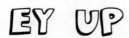

Yorkshire

Hello.

"Ey up Nathan, 'ow are you?"

FECK OFF

Ireland

Go away. Polite f**k off.

"Just feck off will ya Nathan."

GAN CANNY

Newcastle / Sunderland

Take care, farewell. Geordie version of bon voyage.

"Gan canny bonny lad."

GARAGE

Birmingham

Petrol station.

"Seen the prices at the garage? Robbers!"

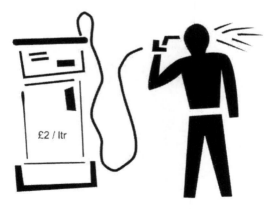

GEET WALLA

Newcastle / Sunderland

Very very big.

"There's a geet walla queue at Tesco, gan go Asda instead."

GEGGIN' IN

Liverpool

Being nosey.

"Nathan was geggin' in to our conversation."

GINGER

Scotland

A soft drink. Pop or soda.

"I need a bottle of ginger."

GIP

Yorkshire

Almost throw up.

"Your face is making me gip Nathan."

GIVE OVER

Yorkshire

Behave.

"Give over Nathan, I don't want to touch your feet."

GIVE YOUR 'EAD A WOBBLE

Manchester

You need to rethink that.

"That's clearly a jelly. Go give your 'ead a wobble."

GIZ A BAG O' CRISPS

Newcastle / Sunderland

A way of saying you don't fancy someone.

"What ya think of that lass Emma?"
"Giz a bag o' crisps man."

GOBSHITE

Liverpool

Loud-mouthed person who talks a lot but says nothing of value.

"Shut it you little gobshite."

GULLY

Birmingham

An alleyway.

"I'm taking a shortcut through the gully."

HADDAWAY MAN

Newcastle / Sunderland

You must be joking.

"Emma gave me her number."
"Haddaway man!"

HAVNAE A SCOOBY

Scotland

I haven't got a clue.

"What time is it?"
"I havnae a scooby."

HEAD'S CHOCKA

Liverpool

Feeling stressed out.

"Me head's chocka after listening to Emma."

HOME N BARGAIN

Liverpool

Home Bargains (the shop) was originally called Home and Bargain. Living in the past.

"Do you want anything from Home n Bargain?"

HOW, MAN

Newcastle / Sunderland

A firm but gentle Geordie warning.

"How, man! Divvent be winding us up."

HOW'S SHE CUTTIN'

Ireland

Greeting – How are you?

"How's she cuttin' today?"

ICE POP

Yorkshire

An ice lolly.

"Nathan is fetching me an ice pop from the shop."

I'LL DO IT NOW IN A MINUTE

Wales

Welsh oxymoron suggesting you will do it in a minute but you certainly will not.

"Do the dishes Nathan."
"I'll do it now in a minute."

ISLAND

Birmingham

A roundabout you find in a road.

"Take the first left at the island."

JESSIE

Scotland

Wimp, wuss or scaredy cat.

"Don't be such a Jessie."

JOBBY

Scotland

Poo.

"You canny polish a jobby."

KEGS

Yorkshire

Trousers

"Nathan you have a stain on your kegs.
I'm not washing them for you again."

KEKS

Yorkshire

Underwear.

"Nathan pure browned his keks last night. It went through to his kegs."

KIRBY KISS

Liverpool

Head butt in the face.

"Nathan was getting on Emma's nerves so she gave him a Kirby Kiss."

KOPITE

Liverpool

Liverpool Football Club (LFC) fan.

"Nathan is a die hard Kopite."

LAMP

Yorkshire / Manchester

Punch or hit.

"Nathan I'll lamp you one if you don't get a move on."

LECHYD DA

Wales

Cheers! Used as a drinking toast. Meaning health in Wales.

"Lechyd da!"

LECKY

Liverpool

Electric.

"Nathan's advice to save on the lecky is
to turn off the lights and sit in the
dark."

LETS AVE IT

Manchester

An exclamation of joy.

"Yes, lets ave it!"

LIKE

Generic term to add to any given word.

"Get on this like, I was chatting to Nathan like, then he fell asleep like."

LIST NOW

Wales

Added before saying
something.

"List now, I'm going to say something."

LOLLY ICE

Liverpool

An ice lolly.

"I'm getting a lolly ice from the ice cream van."

LUG 'OLE

Ear.

"Clean your lug 'oles Nathan because you never seem to hear me."

LUSH

Wales

To describe something lovely.

"Your outfit is lush."

MACKEM

A person from Sunderland or someone who supports the Sunderland football team.

"Nathan is a Mackem, not a Magpie."

MAD FER IT

Manchester

Very excited about something.

"I'm mad fer it tonight."

MAGPIES

Nickname for Newcastle United, named for their black and white stripes.

"Did you watch the Magpies beat Sunderland on derby day?"

MAN

Newcastle / Sunderland

A form of address that can be confusingly used for both men and women.

"Howay man, woman, man. Nathan is confused man!"

ME

Manchester

Used at the end of any sentence about yourself.

"I'm working dead hard, me."

MESSAGES

Ireland

Shopping.

"See you in hour, need to collect the messages first."

MORTAL

Newcastle / Sunderland

Very drunk.

"Emma is away so I'm gannin the toon the neet to get mortal."

NA

Newcastle / Sunderland

No. The opposite of yes.

"Are ye gannin down the pub the neet?"
"Na I went yesterday and got mortal."

NAH THEN

Yorkshire

Hello.

"Nah then young lad."

NEE

Newcastle / Sunderland

No, referring to the amount of something.

"There's nee milk left in the old cow."

NETTY

Newcastle / Sunderland

Toilet.

"Had a few many bottles o; broon and I'm busting, where's ya netty?"

NUTT'N

Liverpool

Scouse for nothing.

"What are you up to tonight Nathan?"
"Emma says we're doing nutt'n."

OCH

Scotland

Expression for swearing OR
surprise OR to add emphasis.

"Och no! My computer has crashed."

OFF FOR A QUICK ONE

Manchester

Usually means one pint but in Manchester a day long drinking session.

"I'm off for a quick one."

ON YA HONKAS

Newcastle / Sunderland

On all fours.

"Get on ya honkas Emma."

ONE BOMB

Birmingham

Knock someone out with one punch.

"He looked at my girlfriend so I had to one bomb him."

OUTDOOR

Birmingham

Off-licence.

"ASDA is shut so I'm going the outdoor for some mushy peas."

OVER BY THERE

Wales

Something is never there or
over there in Wales.

*"It's not over there or by there. It's over
by there."*

'OW MUCH

Yorkshire

A way of expressing something is too expensive.

"'Ow much!? In a bit."

OZZY

Liverpool

Hospital.

"They had to take Nathan the ozzy la."

PAGGERED

Newcastle / Sunderland

Exhausted.

"Eee I'm paggered man."

PANTS

Manchester

Bad or rubbish.

"There's nowt on tv, it's pants."

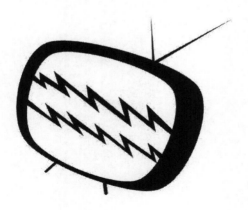

PATTER

Scotland

Banter, chat.

"She was a hacket but I got off with her because her patter was excellent."

PECK ME 'EAD

Manchester

Being annoying

"Shut up, you're pecking me 'ead in."

PET

Newcastle / Sunderland

A term of endearment used in the same way as my love or dear.

"Come and have a cuddle pet."

PIECE

A slice of bread.

"Have a piece with your soup."

PROPA

Very significantly.

"Ye looking propa bonnie the neet Emma."

PURE

Scotland

Really or a lot.

"Scotland is pure class."

PUT WOOD INT' HOLE

Yorkshire

Close the door.

"Thanks for the pop but how many times Nathan; Put wood int' hole. It is freezing!"

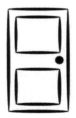

RANK

Yorkshire / Manchester

Disgusting.

"That smell is rank Nathan."

RAPID

Ireland

A wonderful time.

"Ahh last night was rapid man."

RED

Manchester

Manchester United supporter.

"Stay away from him, he's a red."

REEKS

Yorkshire

Smells bad.

"Nathan your feet reek of rotten eggs."

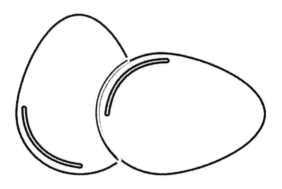

SCENES

An unbelievable or funny
event.

*"Nathan got attacked by Buster.
Absolute scenes!"*

SCOLLOP

Yorkshire

A slice of potato in batter deep fried.

"A scallop butty with ketchup please."

SCOUSE

A stew traditionally made from leftover meat OR the Liverpool accent.

"Nathan has a strong Scouse accent when he eats scouse."

SCOUSER

Someone who is from
Liverpool.

*"Eh? Eh? Eh? Scousers do do dat dough
don't dey dough."*

SHITHOUSE

Liverpool

Someone with no morals and
no regard for anyone else.

"You're such a shithouse Nathan."

SHY BAIRNS GET NOWT

Newcastle / Sunderland

If you don't ask, you don't get.

"Ye think I should ask that lass out?"
"Aye, shy bairns get nowt."

SLÁINTE

Ireland

Used as a drinking toast.
Meaning health in Irish.

"Sláinte!"

SOUND

Liverpool

Cool, good, brilliant, fantastic, great, ace, wonderful, boss.

"This surround sound is sound."

SOZ

Manchester

Short for sorry.

"I didn't know that was your drink, soz. I'll get you another."

SPITTIN

Manchester

Fine rain.

"It's spittin outside, you'll get soaked."

SQUARE GO

Scotland

The Scottish call to fight.

"You're pis*ing me off, square go the now!"

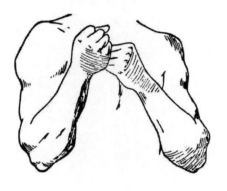

STEAMIN'

Liverpool

Horny.

"Emma was steaming even though there was no milk for coffee."

STEAMIN'

Scotland

Drunk.

"She was steamin' last night."

STOP YA CHATTIN'

Manchester

Stop talking a load of rubbish.

"Do you ever stop ya chattin'?"

STOTTIE

Newcastle / Sunderland

A delicious bread bun.

"Ham and peas pudding stottie for me bait, mint."

SUMMAT

Something.

"Ye got summat stuck in your teeth Nathan."

SUNLUN

Sunderland.

"Nathan is from Sunlun."

SWEAR DOWN

Manchester

I am telling the truth.

"I swear down I'm not a liar."

TARA A BIT

Birmingham

Goodbye.

"Tara a bit, see you tomorrow."

TEA CAKE

Yorkshire

A bread roll (bap or bun).

"Gimme that tea cake, I'm hungry."

TELL ME NOW

Wales

Used before asking a question.

"Tell me now, what is the meaning of life?"

THE ASDA

ASDA.

"I need to go the ASDA before I go home."

TIN TIN TIN

Yorkshire

It isn't in the tin.

"I've checked and it tin tin tin."

TRAINEES

Liverpool

Trainers.

"Going to town to get some new trainees later."

TWONK

Yorkshire

An idiot.

"You're a twonk Nathan, do one."

US

Me.

"Give us a kiss pet."

WEY EYE MAN

Newcastle / Sunderland

Yes.

"Is Newcastle better than Sunderland?"
"Wey eye man!"

WHERE YOU TO?

Wales

Where are you?

"Where you to Emma?"

WHILE

Until.

"I'm working 6 while 8 tomorrow while you call me a Wazzok."

YAM

Birmingham

A person from the neighboring Black Country.

"He pretends he's from Brum but he's from Dudley. The Yam!"

YE BLEEDIN' DOPE YA

Ireland

You're the least clever person I have ever met. Silly Billy.

"Don't lick that. Ye bleedin' dope ya."

YEE

Newcastle / Sunderland

You.

"Yee can larn yorsel a few words here if yee can understand us."

YE WHA?

Liverpool

You what? Hearing but not believing someone had the audacity to say or do something. An elevated version of pardon.

"Nathan legged it, the blert."
"Ye Wha??"

YORKSHIRE PUDDING

A pudding traditionally served with a Sunday roast.

"I can't wait for Sunday to taste Emma's delicious Yorkshire puddings."

YORKSHIRE TEA

The most popular tea sold in the UK, based in Harrogate.

"Put t' kettle on and have nice a cup of Yorkshire tea with me."

YOUS

Liverpool

Plural of you. Means "you"
when addressing a group of
people that you are speaking to.

*"Yous are doing my head in. I'm going
back to Emma."*

TR'A

TR'A

TR'A

TR'A

TR'A

TR'A

Printed in Great Britain
by Amazon